POLISH *Classic* DESSERTS

POLISH *Classic* DESSERTS

LAURA & PETER ZERANSKI
PHOTOGRAPHY BY BOB ROCK

PELICAN PUBLISHING COMPANY

GRETNA 2013

ISBN 978-1-45561-726-5

Printed in China

Published by Pelican Publishing Company, Inc.
1000 Burmaster Street, Gretna, Louisiana 70053

We dedicate this book to the memory of all Polish people who were driven from their homeland, assimilated into new cultures, thrived, and stayed connected to their roots by sharing these heritage traditions and flavors.

CONTENTS

INTRODUCTION

Poles love desserts! We love to eat and we certainly love our sweet endings. With this book, our second, we continue the journey of sharing heritage Polish dishes, focusing on the desserts that you may remember from your Mama's or Babcia's kitchen. On these pages you'll find many favorites traditionally associated with holidays such as Christmas and Easter, as well as desserts that are especially quick and easy to prepare on a busy day. You'll find desserts that are casual or rustic, and desserts that are incredibly elegant – appropriate for the fanciest dinner party. Each has been extensively tested in our home kitchen (to the delight of family, friends and neighbors) to make sure you can prepare them successfully in your home kitchen. The guesswork of imprecise measurements has been taken out but all the love you need to make your guests or family rave at your culinary prowess has been left in. It's all about their smiles!

Polish desserts are generally less sweet than many of the desserts we see and taste in America. Many recipes in this book take advantage of the natural sweetness from fresh fruits such as plums, berries or tart apples, and of natural flavorings such as honey, nuts, cinnamon or semi-sweet chocolate. Many of the sweets are heavily associated with specific holidays because they traditionally relied on seasonal produce and flavorings only available at certain times of the year. These restrictions of seasonality are now relegated to days of long ago as the buying power of large modern grocery chains reaches all corners of the globe, regardless of when or where produce comes from.

As we were reviewing the vast library of classic Polish desserts clamoring to appear in our book, we wanted to pick the ones that have been most traditional and popular over generations, ones that you could make successfully, ones that represented a good cross-section of types and, most importantly, the ones that would have the biggest "WOW factor" coming out of your kitchen. We only included recipes for which ingredients are readily available at most large grocery chains.

Most of these recipes were originated generations ago by great-grandmothers who cooked by "feel." Little was documented, so the handwritten, food-stained, kitchen-worn notes we were lovingly lent were often sketchy (at best) because these talented cooks eyeballed a lot of the ingredients. That's where Laura's testing came in because she made each dessert enough times to make sure each chosen recipe met her high standards and could be a winner for most home dessert makers.

We ended up with 45 different desserts, plus a number of variations that take advantage of seasonal ingredients. We arranged them in somewhat natural groups: *Mazurkas* (layers of a shortbread type of dough, filled with fruits, nuts or icings); *Babas* (yeast-risen cakes traditional for holidays); Cookies (crumbly and full of subtle flavors); Tortes (spectacular European cakes that are sometimes flourless, sometimes rich and decadent, but always amazing); other Cakes, delectable Pastries; and a handful of other very special desserts that didn't fit comfortably into any logical category, but which were much too good to be omitted.

These are the desserts we love, these are the desserts we grew up with, these are the desserts you've been requesting, and these are the most popular desserts you'll go back to, over and over again. ***Smacznego!*** *(Bon Appétit in Polish)*

Laura and Peter Zeranski

Traditions and Desserts

No traditional holiday feast is complete without a sweet ending. For many Poles, their earliest childhood recollections are of the delicious food of those holidays, and especially the desserts. They make such a strong impression on all the senses that those memories stay with them their entire lives. One of Peter's earliest childhood memories is of waiting at a white picket fence for his father to come home from work on Christmas Eve (*Wigilia* in Polish). He was perhaps four years old and the memory of that one glorious, celebratory evening has stayed in the depths of his mind for six decades.

The aromas from the kitchen are intoxicating. The table is set, along with the traditional empty chair reserved for a traveler, an unexpected guest who may need shelter and food on a cold winter night. The feast is ready but Peter is outside searching the darkening sky for the first star, symbolic of the star of Bethlehem which guided the Three Kings to Bethlehem.

The feast begins with the sharing of the *Opłatek*, a rectangle of thin, unleavened dough, like a communion wafer, stamped with scenes of the Nativity and blessed when possible. Everyone shares a piece with everyone else while exchanging best wishes for this holiday and for the coming year.

After the blessing, everyone starts passing platters. The meal is meatless and the Christmas Eve menu in Peter's family has remained pretty much the same for several generations: clear *Barszcz* (Beet Soup) or Dried Mushroom Soup, a fish dish such as herring or carp, Crepes with Mushroom and Sauerkraut, Noodles with Poppy Seeds. There is no room on the table for more dishes.

No Christmas Eve supper can be complete without the huge array of desserts Peter remembers, many of which are in this collection: Kolachki (page 33), Angel Wing Crisps (page 34), Warsaw Fruit Cake (page 46), a classic Holiday Gingerbread Cake (page 53), Grandma's Cheesecake (page 62), usually a Nut Roll or a Poppy Seed Roll (page 74) and always for tradition's sake, Dried Fruit Compote (page 81).

The family gathers around the Christmas tree, sings carols and then opens gifts. Peter's parents love the Polish carols of their childhoods, but their vinyl records, sent from Poland, are now old and very scratchy. He endures the singing, sitting impatiently, until the big trash bag finally appears (for discarded wrapping paper) and he is invited to begin distributing gifts. The electric train, with its flashing headlight and piercing whistle, is a huge hit. Finally the evening is over after the family returns home from midnight Mass. Sleep comes slowly.

In the Spring comes Easter – one of the two biggest dessert opportunities of the year. Peter's memories of Easter celebrations go back just as far as his Christmas memories, but are treasured not for the gifts but for the classic Easter desserts he loves so much.

Certainly Easter is a religious celebration, but it is also a celebration of foods often experienced only once a year. Cooking and baking begins days and even weeks ahead of time. Intricate decorations grace the sweet baked goods. On Palm Sunday, tall, thin branches of pussy willow are blessed because palm trees are not indigenous to Poland. On the Saturday before Easter, the table is set and in the center rests a little sugar or butter lamb, a symbol of Jesus with a small, red sash around its neck. Samples of the Easter dishes are put in a basket and taken to the Polish church to be blessed. Inside are colored eggs, salt, kielbasa, ham, slices of Baba, Mazurka, Cheesecake and the other desserts.

Served after Mass on Easter Sunday, the big feast is actually a sumptuous cold luncheon. Family and friends gather around the table. Just as at Christmas Eve with the *Opłatek*, everyone shares pieces of egg with everyone else and exchanges best wishes for peace, good health and happiness. There are too many dishes to fit on the dining room table. It's an endless banquet of traditional foods such as hardboiled eggs, baked ham, kielbasa, sliced turkey or pork loin, *Ćwikła* (the iconic garnish of chopped beets and horseradish), fish in aspic, vegetable salad, and more.

No Easter feast can be complete without several desserts, including many from the pages that follow: several Mazurkas – the beautiful, decorated shortbread cakes (pages 13-17), an Easter Baba (page 22), a light and fluffy Easter Cheesecake (page 58), or a platter of Papal Crème Cakes (page 73).

In these days of a healthier consciousness, desserts are enjoyed in moderation, but they're always good for the soul and the ones prepared classically for special days keep Polish heritage strong and vibrant.

ROYAL MAZURKA
Mazurek Królewski

Mazurkas are festive Polish cakes traditionally served at Easter. They are usually decorated with beautiful Easter-themed designs on top. And they come in endless flavors, some filled with a fruit spread between layers, some iced with chocolate, some topped with a sweet meringue, some containing dried fruit and nuts in the dough, but they're all delicious. This Royal Mazurka has been a favorite through the ages.

YIELDS 32 squares

DOUGH
6 eggs
2 2/3 cups confectioners' sugar
1/2 cup boiling water
3 tablespoons lemon juice
zest of one lemon
3 1/4 cups flour
1 teaspoon almond extract
3/4 cup almonds, ground
1 1/2 cups butter, melted
zest of one lemonbutter for pans

Preheat oven to 375°F. Line two 9x13 baking pans with wax or parchment paper and butter the paper *(Note: butter is best since sprays or oils will change the taste).*

Beat the eggs with the confectioners' sugar using standing or handheld mixer at high speed for 5-7 minutes until pale yellow and very light. Mix the water, lemon juice, zest, and almond extract in a small bowl or cup. Add to the egg and sugar mixture in a thin stream while continuing to beat for 3-5 minutes. Combine the almonds with the flour. Fold flour mixture, alternating with the melted butter, into the egg mixture. Mix lightly to incorporate.

Divide batter in 2 equal halves (approximately 6 cups) and fold into the prepared baking pans. Bake 20-25 minutes or until edges turn golden brown. Watch carefully to ensure edges do not burn.

Cool for about 10 minutes, remove from pans and place on rack to cool completely.

(recipe continued at right)

(recipe continued from left)

SPREAD
1 cup apricot jam

ICING
2 cups confectioners' sugar
1 tablespoon warm water
2-3 tablespoons lemon juice

Mix the water and 2 tablespoons lemon juice with confectioners' sugar until sugar dissolves and mixture is white, smooth and coats the back of the spoon. Add more sugar if icing is too thin or more lemon juice if icing is too thick.

Spread one cooled cake with the apricot jam. Cover with the second cake. Spread the top with the icing. Allow icing to harden before cutting into small squares for serving.

Cake can be decorated with almonds and apricots.

Note: store in the fridge and serve well chilled to prevent the apricot jam from running.

Gypsy Mazurka
Mazurek Cyganski

YIELDS about 48 pieces

3/4 cup raisins	zest of 1 lemon
3/4 cup sliced figs	6 tablespoons cornstarch
3/4 cup sliced dates	5 eggs, separated
3/4 cup sliced candied orange rind	7 tablespoons sugar
2 1/4 cups chopped walnuts	1 teaspoon vanilla extract

Preheat oven to 350°F. Mix the fruit, nuts, rind and zest with the cornstarch and set aside.

Beat the egg whites until they form stiff peaks. Add the sugar a tablespoon at a time. Add the egg yolks and the vanilla.

Fold the fruit mixture into the egg mixture and mix slightly.

Butter and flour a 12x15-inch cake pan. Spread batter over the prepared cake pan and bake for 20 minutes.

Remove from oven and let cool. Cut into small 2-inch squares or triangles.

Candied Orange Rind
Kandyzowana Skórka Pomarańczowa

Oranges, cleaned and peeled
Sugar
Water

Put orange peels in a sauce pan with enough cold water to cover. Boil for 10 minutes and drain. Cover again with cold water and repeat the cycle 2 more times. Drain the rinds and rinse with cold water. Scrape off the pithy white part of the peel and cut into very thin strips.

Measure the volume of orange rind strips. For each cup of rind, in a sauce pan prepare a sugar syrup of 1 cup sugar to 1 cup water. Add the rind to the syrup and cook low and slow until syrup is completely absorbed. Be patient. This process takes several hours. Stir the mixture occasionally. Be vigilant near the end of the process to prevent burning.

Cool the rind strips on wax or parchment paper. Coat the strips with granulated sugar. Dry strips overnight on a rack. The sugared peel will keep for several months in an airtight container.

WALNUT MAZURKA
Mazurek Orzechowy

The name *mazurka* came from Frederick Chopin's music. This great Polish composer was born in a small village in the Polish province of *Mazury*, where a local folk dance, the *mazurek*, had originated. This dance was very popular throughout Europe in the 19th century. Chopin loved his homeland so much that he incorporated many themes of the *mazurek* into his compositions. And so Poles who loved Chopin's music honored him by naming their favorite Easter cake after his compositions. It's not everyone who has a cake named after them.

YIELDS about 48 pieces

DOUGH
2/3 cup soft butter
2 3/4 cups sifted flour
2/3 cup confectioners' sugar
2 teaspoons baking powder
1 egg
1 egg yolk
1/4 cup sour cream

Cut the butter into the flour using a knife and rub the butter in with your fingertips, or use a standing mixer on low speed mix until dough resembles course crumbs. Add sugar and baking powder and mix. Add the remaining ingredients. Knead the dough until it leaves the sides of the bowl and forms a ball. Refrigerate in a covered dish for 30 minutes.

Remove dough from refrigerator and roll into a 12x15-inch rectangle. Place dough in a 12x15 pan and spread until the pan is covered. Bake in a 375°F oven for 10 minutes. Remove from the oven and set aside. Lower the oven temperature to 350°F.

WALNUT SPREAD
1/2 cup unsalted butter
3 egg yolks
2 tablespoons lemon juice
2 cups confectioners' sugar
1 teaspoon vanilla extract
1 cup flour
2 cups walnuts, ground

Beat the butter with the egg yolks using either a standing or handheld mixer for 10 minutes. Gradually add the lemon juice, confectioners' sugar and vanilla. Add the flour and nuts alternately. Spread evenly on top of the prebaked dough.

(recipe continued at right)

(recipe continued from left)
MERINGUE
2 egg whites
1 cup confectioners' sugar
1 teaspoon vanilla extract

Beat the egg whites until they form stiff peaks. Add the confectioners' sugar and vanilla gradually while continuing to beat. Spread over the nut mixture.

Bake in a 350°F oven for 25 to 30 minutes, or until the meringue starts to turn golden. Remove from oven and cool. Cut into small 2-inch squares or triangles.

Saffron Baba
Babka Szafranowa

YIELDS 2 Babas, about 32 slices, depending on thickness

DOUGH

3/4 cup dark rum	1 cup cream
3/4 cup raisins	1/2 teaspoon saffron
4 1/2 teaspoons dry active yeast	1 teaspoon vanilla extract
1 tablespoon sugar	1 teaspoon salt
1/2 cup lukewarm water	zest of 1 lemon
6 cups flour	zest of 1 orange
8 egg yolks	3/4 cup butter, softened
2 whole eggs	3/4 cup candied orange rind (page 14)
1 cup sugar	

One to three days before making the baba, soak the raisins in the dark rum. Drain any excess liquid and toss raisins in a small amount of flour to ensure they will not sink to the bottom of the batter.

Dissolve yeast and the tablespoon of sugar in lukewarm water. Cover and set in warm place until yeast begins to bubble.

In the bowl of a standing mixer, using the paddle attachment, beat egg yolks and whole eggs together until thickened. Gradually add the cup of sugar and continue beating until well combined. Stir in the cream, yeast mixture, saffron, salt, vanilla and lemon and orange zests. Gradually add flour to make a soft dough. Change paddle to a dough hook and knead until smooth. Add the softened butter and continue to knead until the butter is worked in well. Add the rum-soaked raisins and the candied orange rind and knead until dough is no longer sticky.

Place dough in a greased bowl, turning to coat all sides with grease. Cover bowl and set in a warm place until dough has doubled in size. Punch dough down and divide into two 9-inch bundt or tube pans greased and floured. Place in a warm place until dough doubles in size.

Preheat oven to 350°F. Bake the babas for 10 minutes. Lower the oven temperature to 300°F and bake for an additional 35-45 minutes until golden brown and skewer inserted in the center comes out clean. Cover with foil to prevent the top from browning too quickly.

Remove from oven and let cool for 10 minutes. Invert onto a plate and lift off the pan.

(recipe continued at left)

(recipe continued from right)

GLAZE

2 cup confectioners' sugar
2 tablespoon lemon juice or rum
2 tablespoon water

Mix confectioners' sugar, lemon juice (or rum) and water. Drizzle over the top of the cake. Garnish with pieces of candied orange rind.

SAND BABA
Babka Piaskowa

This is the most traditional and basic of babas from among dozens of varieties. It is both fluffy and somewhat fragile, crumbling at a heavy touch. It's surprisingly moist, and enhanced with the subtle aroma of vanilla and almond. Perfect for afternoon tea, a traditional Polish snack time, as a not-too-sweet flavor sparkler, with a cup of hot tea or coffee.

SERVES 8-10

1/3 cup butter, softened
3/4 cup sugar
4 eggs
4 tablespoons plain yogurt
1 teaspoon almond extract
1 teaspoon vanilla extract
1 1/2 cups flour
2 teaspoons baking powder

Cream the butter with the sugar using a standing mixer. Add the eggs one at a time, beating at high speed. Add the yogurt, almond and vanilla extracts and beat 3 more minutes. Add the flour and baking powder and beat 5 more minutes.

Grease a 9-inch bundt or tube pan well or spray the pan with a commercial baking spray. Spoon the batter into the prepared pan, spreading the batter so the sides are higher than the center.

Bake at 350°F for 40-45 minutes until the cake begins to pull away from the sides of the pan and a toothpick inserted in the center comes out clean.

Transfer the pan to a wire rack and cool for 15 minutes.

Place a plate over the top of the pan and invert the pan onto the plate and lift the pan.

Dust the baba with confectioners' sugar before serving.

Easter Baba
Babka Wielkanocna

YIELDS 16 slices

DOUGH
4 1/2 teaspoons active dry yeast
2/3 cup sugar
1 cup light cream, warm
4 cups flour, sifted
6 egg yolks
2 teaspoons vanilla
2 tablespoons lemon zest
2 tablespoons orange zest
1/2 cup butter, melted
1/2 cup raisins
1/2 cup slivered almonds, chopped

Cover raisins with boiling water, let steep for 5-10 minutes and drain.

Combine yeast and 2 tablespoons of the sugar in a bowl. Mix in the cream and let stand for 5 minutes. Mix in 1 cup of the flour and let stand in a warm place until doubled in size.

Using a standing mixer, beat the egg yolks with the rest of the sugar until fluffy. Add the rest of the flour, the yeast mixture, vanilla, and orange and lemon zests and mix until well combined. Switch beaters to a dough hook and knead dough for 5 minutes. Add the butter in small portions and knead until dough is smooth. Add raisins and almonds and knead some more.

Grease a 9-inch bundt or tube pan well or spray pan with a commercial baking spray. Arrange the dough evenly in the pan. Place in a warm place to rise until doubled in size, about 1 hour.

Bake in a 350°F oven for 35-40 minutes or until toothpick inserted comes out clean.

Transfer the pan to a wire rack and cool for 15 minutes.

Place a plate over the top of the pan and invert the pan onto the plate and lift the pan.

GLAZE
1 cup confectioners' sugar
1 tablespoon lemon juice
1 tablespoon water

Mix confectioners' sugar, lemon juice and water. Drizzle over the top of the cake.

FILLED BABY BABAS
Babeczki Smietankowe

Serve these to your guests on a pretty platter and they won't believe these little delights weren't born in a bakery. They are just fun – fun to make, fun to admire and fun to eat. It's a good way to introduce kids to a traditional Easter dessert.

YIELDS 12-15 pieces, depending on the size of the pan

DOUGH
2 cups butter
2 3/4 cups flour, sifted
2/3 cup confectioners' sugar
4 egg yolks
1 teaspoon vanilla

In the bowl of a standing mixer, using the paddle, cut the butter into the flour until it forms coarse crumbs. Combine with sugar. Add the egg yolks and vanilla. Change to the dough hook, knead the dough until it forms a ball. Wrap ball in plastic wrap and refrigerate for 10 minutes.

CREAM
2 eggs
2 egg yolks
2/3 cup sugar
1 teaspoon vanilla extract
2 tablespoons cornstarch
2 cups light cream, hot

Beat the eggs and egg yolks with the sugar for 5 minutes. Add the vanilla and cornstarch. Beat some more. Continue to beat while slowly pouring in the hot cream.

Cook mixture on low heat, stirring constantly until it thickens. Cool.

Roll out the dough to about 1/4 inch thickness. Cut out circles large enough to line a standard muffin cup. Line the inside of one muffin cup with one circle of dough.

Fill the dough-lined muffin cups about 1/3 full with cream mixture. Cover each cup with another dough circle and seal edges.

Bake in a 400°F oven for 20 minutes until golden brown. Gently turn out the baby babas. Dust them with confectioners' sugar before serving.

ALMOND COOKIES
Ciasteczka Migdałowe

Poles love to entertain and quite often company will be invited for coffee (or tea) in the middle of the afternoon. Peter's parents enjoyed entertaining friends on Sunday afternoons. It was easy to prepare something hospitable, the bottles of vodka and wine stayed corked, and the guests never stayed too long! In the 1950s, most of their friends had recently emigrated from Poland, so the main topics of discussion were often quite political. The women always wore dresses. The men always wore jackets and ties. Music was always playing on the Hi-Fi – usually pre-war ballads from back home. Coffee or tea was served with platters of cookies or other small, casual baked goods.

These delicate, little almond delicacies were often served because their subtle almond flavor was a great accompaniment to a dish of ice cream or mousse, or delicious just plain with a cup of coffee.

YIELDS 5 dozen

1/2 pound unsalted butter, softened
1 3/4 cups flour, sifted
2/3 cup confectioners' sugar, sifted
1 teaspoon almond extract
1 teaspoon vanilla extract
1 cup almonds, ground

Using a standing mixer, mix the butter into the flour until it resembles coarse breadcrumbs. Add the sugar, and the almond and vanilla flavorings. Mix the dough until well incorporated. Add the almonds and mix.

Preheat the oven to 450°F. Line a cookie sheet with parchment paper. Roll the dough to 1/8 inch thickness. Cut into 2-inch squares or circles. Bake for 8 minutes until golden brown.

CHESTNUTS
Kasztanki

What Peter and Laura find particularly noteworthy about these little chocolate morsels is the texture of the finished cookie. It is very light and fragile, so if you only bite in halfway, the cookie tends to crumble. Roll them out like marbles, small enough to be one-bite wonders.

YIELDS 3 dozen

2/3 cup sweet butter, softened
1 teaspoon vanilla
3 tablespoons sugar
1 cup flour
1 cup ground walnuts
1/2 cup cocoa powder
1/2 cup confectioners' sugar

Preheat oven to 375°F.

Using a standing mixer, beat the butter with the vanilla and sugar for approximately 5 minutes. Combine the flour with the walnuts in a separate bowl. Add in small batches to the butter bowl and mix until combined well.

Roll dough into marble-sized balls. Place the balls on a parchment-lined cookie sheet about 2 inches apart and bake for 15 minutes.

Combine the cocoa and confectioners' sugar. Roll the slightly warm cookies in the mixture.

Cookies can be stored in an airtight container.

GINGER HEARTS IN CHOCOLATE
Pierniczki w Czekoladzie

Polish *Pierniczki* are quite similar to American gingerbread cookies, but they are not shaped like little men. Instead, they are usually heart-shaped, dipped in chocolate and decorated with icing. They are very popular in Poland during the holidays and have a long history dating back to the Middle Ages. One very old tradition in Poland is to hang them on the Christmas tree. Using a plastic straw, make a small hole in each cookie before baking. Later, thread a thin ribbon through the hole in the cookie to hang it on your tree. This is a great project to do with the kids.

YIELDS approximately 5 dozen, depending on the size of your cookie cutter

DOUGH
Prepare the same dough as for Holiday Gingerbread Cake on page 53.

Preheat the oven to 350°F. Roll out the dough to 1/4 inch thickness. Using a cookie cutter, cut dough into hearts, stars or other holiday shapes. Place the cut shapes on a parchment-lined cookie sheet and bake for 7 minutes.

ICING
4 ounces chocolate, semi-sweet morsels
1/3 cup light cream
1/4 cup confectioners' sugar

Heat the cream in a medium saucepan to just boiling. Remove from the heat and add the chocolate. Let sit for a minute and then whisk until chocolate is melted and smooth. Add the confectioners' sugar and mix well. Spread over the cookies. Let cookies set until the icing dries and then store in an airtight container for a few days to let the spices thoroughly do their work. Before serving, decorate with icing designs, if desired.

Hint: these cookies freeze well.

KOLACHKI
Kołaczki

Kolachki are extremely versatile and among the prettiest and most colorful little cookies to ever grace your Christmas dessert platter. Their origins are claimed by several Eastern European bakers, notably the Slovaks, and Croatians. But regardless of how one spells their name, they are absolutely delicious. Kolachki can be square, diamond-shaped, or have all four corners tucked into the center to make a cute little envelope. The dough can be made with cream cheese, sour cream or yeast. Fillings are usually fruit jams, nut paste or sweet cheese. Laura tested several kinds but her and Peter's favorite was this traditional flaky version made with cream cheese dough and filled with apricot, raspberry or prune jam. And what makes them especially "host-friendly" is that you can freeze a batch of unbaked, filled Kolachki for later. Bake them frozen.

YIELDS 5 dozen

8 ounces cream cheese, softened	fruit jam for fillings, your choice
3/4 pound of butter, softened	1 egg white
3 cups flour	confectioners' sugar, enough for dusting

Using a standing mixer, beat the cream cheese and butter at medium-high speed for about 3 minutes (or if using a handheld mixer, for about 6 minutes) until light and creamy.

Reduce mixer speed to low and add flour, 1 cup at a time, until combined.

Divide the dough into 4 equal parts and wrap each part in plastic wrap. Refrigerate dough for at least 1 hour. Preheat oven to 350°F.

Between 2 sheets of floured wax or parchment paper, roll out one portion of the dough (keeping the remaining dough refrigerated until ready to roll) to ¼ inch thickness. Remove the top paper and cut the dough into 2-inch squares using a square cookie or biscuit cutter. If you don't have a cutter, just cut dough with a knife into 2-inch strips lengthwise and then again widthwise to make 2-inch squares.

Using a very small spoon, place less than half a teaspoon of jam in the center of each square. Brush 2 opposite corners with egg white. Fold one corner over the filling, then overlap the second corner and gently pinch corners to seal. Repeat with the remaining two corners. Corners must be securely sealed or they will come apart while baking. *(Note: avoid putting too much filling into the cookie, otherwise the jam will run out too much while baking).*

Arrange cookies on a parchment-lined cookie sheet 2 inches apart. Bake for 15 minutes or until golden. Allow to cool. Dust with confectioners' sugar just before serving.

If the finished cookies are to be served later, they can be stored without confectioners' sugar between sheets of wax or parchment paper in an airtight container.

ANGEL WING CRISPS
Chruściki

These light, delicacies are a favorite way to end any festive meal but for many Poles bring back wonderful memories from traditional holidays such as Christmas Eve or Easter. They are very elegant, making them a perfect way to show off your skills. The dough itself is not sweet; most of the sweetness comes from the powdered sugar sprinkled on just before serving. Occasionally they can be purchased commercially but when made at home with loving hands, they are oh so much lighter because of all the kneading, which injects air into the dough. Pile them high and watch them disappear.

YIELDS 7 to 8 dozen

6 egg yolks	1 teaspoon lemon zest
1 whole egg	1 teaspoon orange zest
3 tablespoons sugar	2 1/4 cups flour
3 tablespoons sour cream	1/4 teaspoon baking powder
2 teaspoon light rum, vodka, or vinegar	1/2 teaspoon salt
1 teaspoon vanilla	3/4 cup vegetable oil for frying
1 teaspoon orange extract	3/4 cup confectioners' sugar
1 teaspoon lemon extract	Additional flour for kneading

Cream the egg yolks and whole egg with the sugar. Add the sour cream, rum, vanilla, orange and lemon extracts and zest and mix until smooth.

Sift the flour, baking powder and salt together. Mix into the egg mixture a little at a time to make stiff dough.

Turn the dough out onto a floured surface. Knead the dough, keeping it and your surface well floured as you work it. Allow the dough to absorb as much flour as it can until it is no longer sticky.

Separate the dough into smaller portions and roll out very thin - almost transparent.

Cut the dough into strips approximately 1 1/2 inches wide and 4 inches long. Make a one inch slit, lengthwise, toward one end of the strip. Pull the long end of the strip through the slit.

Heat the oil to 375°F. Fry cookies in small batches in the hot oil turning once. The cookies will fry quickly in a minute or less. They should be evenly golden, not brown.

Drain on paper towels or brown paper. When cool, dust with powdered sugar.

Cookies are best when eaten right away. However, they may be stored in air tight containers with wax paper between layers, without any powdered sugar. Dust them with powdered sugar just before serving.

(recipe continued at left)

(recipe continued from right)
Tips: If you don't have a deep fryer, a deep heavy pot containing with 6 or 8 inches of oil will work just as well. Also, using a standing mixer with a dough hook works just as well as hand kneading and is considerably easier.

CHOCOLATE SANDWICH COOKIES
Ciasteczka z Czekoladą

These are irresistible! They aren't hard to make, they taste great and are sure to impress.

Poles everywhere are very social. Visits to friends and family are customary during the holidays but it works both ways because Poles love to entertain as well. Bakers in every circle compete to produce the prettiest and most tasty assortment of goodies. Sometimes, it can get quite competitive! The baking starts in early December and soon boxes and tins of delicacies are lovingly put away for the holiday visits. *"Idziemy na wizite"* ("We're going for a visit") is the frequent call of a Sunday afternoon – Peter remembers quite well his discomfort in getting dressed up and being pulled out the door by his parents to visit their friends. A clean, white shirt and tie was the only acceptable dress code for men and young boys. Most of his parents' friends did not have kids his age to play with, so he was forced to sit in the circle with the adults and was expected to participate in the conversations. Even though he was only 9 or 10 years old, they would dutifully and respectfully keep him involved. He grew to tolerate those conversations but when the *"podwieczorek"* (midafternoon snack similar to high tea in Britain) was served, things always started looking up!

YIELDS 3 dozen

DOUGH

1 stick softened butter	1 egg
2 3/4 cups flour, sifted	2 egg yolks
2/3 cup confectioners' sugar	3 tablespoons sour cream
2 teaspoons baking powder	

In the bowl of a standing mixer, mix the butter with the flour until it resembles coarse crumbs. Add the remaining ingredients and mix until the dough leaves the sides of the bowl to form a ball. Wrap the dough in plastic and refrigerate for at least 15 minutes.

Preheat oven to 375°F. Line a cookie sheet with parchment paper. Roll out the dough to 1/8 inch thick. Cut the dough into rounds using a 1-inch cookie cutter. Place cookie rounds on the parchment-lined cookie sheet and bake for 10 minutes or until golden brown. Cool before filling.

FILLING

2 eggs	1/2 teaspoon vanilla extract
2/3 cup sugar	1 tablespoon vodka
2/3 cup unsalted butter	5 tablespoons cocoa powder

Using a standing mixer, beat the eggs with the sugar until light and fluffy. In a separate bowl, cream the butter. Add the creamed butter to the egg and sugar mixture in

(recipe continued at right)

(recipe continued from left)

small amounts while beating at low speed. Add the rest of the ingredients and mix until well incorporated. Chill filling for at least 30 minutes before spreading on the cookies.

Spread approximately one teaspoon of filling over one cookie round and top with a second round to make a sandwich.

Refrigerate cookies for one hour to allow the filling to stiffen a bit.

MOCHA TORTE
Tort Mokka

This is a very popular Polish recipe because it is easy to prepare, looks impressive on the table, and has memorable flavors. Peter's mother related the story that this torte gained its fame during World War II. Food was very scarce, most of the bakeries were shuttered and many families had no income because the men were fighting the war abroad or imprisoned in camps. Out of desperation, a few ladies "of privilege" who had never worked a day in their lives decided to open a little café and sell the only item they knew how to prepare well – elegant tortes. Under near impossible conditions, they produced exquisite delicacies and the café became famous throughout Warsaw. Years later, one of these ladies immigrated to the United States and shared her original recipe with Peter's mother. There are other versions, but this is the classic.

SERVES 8

BATTER
8 egg whites
2 1/3 cups confectioners' sugar
1 tablespoon lemon juice
2 1/2 cups almonds, ground

Preheat oven to 275°F. Line the bottom of two 9-inch, round cake pans with parchment paper.

Beat egg whites until very stiff. Add sugar by spoonfuls while continuing to beat for 3 more minutes. Add lemon juice and beat an additional 5 minutes. Add the almonds and mix lightly.

Divide batter evenly between the 2 pans. Smooth tops with a spatula. Bake for 1½ hours until the layers are golden brown on top, crisp to the touch but soft inside. When done, a toothpick inserted in the center will come out clean. Remove from oven and cool.

Note: low and slow is the way to go with this one...that's no mistake!

ICING
2 cups unsalted butter, softened
3 egg yolks
2/3 cup confectioners' sugar
3 tablespoons instant espresso coffee
4 1/2 tablespoons vodka

Using a standing mixer, cream the butter, egg yolks and sugar. Dissolve the instant espresso coffee in the vodka. Gradually add the coffee to the creamed mixture.

(recipe continued at left)

(recipe continued from right)
Assemble the torte by spreading the icing between the layers and on top. Refrigerate for a few hours.

To serve, cut with a thin, sharp knife, using a sawing motion.

LEMON TORTE
Tort Cytrynowy

While Laura was testing all the torte recipes and Peter faithfully tasted the results, it became quickly obvious that the bright flavor of this torte makes it an instant and huge success. As you pry away the first bite, making sure your fork jabs into both cake and icing, and lift it smoothly towards your lips, immediately your senses are put on alert that something very special is approaching. And when the first bite is savored, you are in awe at the brightness of the flavor – lemony without being too tart – and the light texture of the cake itself. All senses are just totally awakened and are instantly begging for more.

SERVES 16

BATTER

10 eggs, separated
2 1/2 cups confectioners' sugar
1 tablespoon fresh lemon juice
1 cup flour, sifted
1 cup cornstarch, sifted
 zest of one lemon

Preheat oven to 350°F. Grease three 9-inch, round cake pans, or line the bottoms with wax paper or parchment paper.

Beat the egg yolks with the sugar for 5 minutes. Add the lemon juice. In a separate bowl, beat the egg whites until stiff and fold into the egg and sugar mixture. Add the sifted flour and cornstarch and lemon zest to the egg mixture and mix lightly.

Divide batter evenly among the 3 pans. Bake for 30-35 minutes or until a toothpick inserted in each center comes out clean. Remove from oven and cool completely.

FILLING

1 tablespoon lemon zest
1/2 cup fresh lemon juice
1 tablespoon cornstarch
6 tablespoons butter
3/4 cup sugar
4 egg yolks

In a small bowl, using a whisk, beat the egg yolks until smooth and set aside.

Mix the zest, lemon juice and cornstarch together in a small saucepan until smooth. Add butter and sugar and, stirring constantly, bring to a boil over medium heat. Simmer for 1 minute, stirring constantly.

Whisk a small amount of the hot lemon mixture into the egg yolks. Pour the egg

(recipe continued at right)

(recipe continued from left)

yolk mixture into the saucepan, beating rapidly with the whisk. Reduce the heat to low and continue to cook the mixture, stirring constantly, for 5 minutes or until thickened. Remove from heat.

Place a piece of wax paper or plastic wrap directly on top of the mixture to prevent a skin from forming while it cools. Cool to room temperature and then refrigerate at least 1 hour.

SYRUP

1/2 cup water
3 tablespoons sugar
juice of 2 lemons
1/2 cup vodka

In a small saucepan, bring the water to a boil. Remove from heat. Add the sugar and stir until dissolved. Add the lemon juice and the vodka.

ICING

4 egg yolks
1 1/3 cups confectioners' sugar
4 teaspoons lemon juice
2 sticks unsalted butter, softened

Using a standing mixer, beat the egg yolks with the sugar for 5 minutes. Add the lemon juice and butter in small amounts, beating constantly until stiff and spreadable.

To assemble the torte, sprinkle each layer with the syrup to moisten but not soak. Spread the filling between the layers and stack the layers. Spread the icing over the top and sides. Decorate with candied lemon rind or lemon zest.

POPPY SEED TORTE
Tort Makowy

Poppy seeds are used in many cuisines around the world and they are a key element of many Polish holiday baked goods. They are harvested from opium poppy plants but the seeds themselves do not contain any significant amounts of opiates. They are highly nutritious and, according to popular sources, less allergenic than many seeds and nuts. This torte is both a visual delight and a beautiful marriage of flavors among the vanilla, raspberry jam and poppy seeds, which also add a binding texture. It's a favorite.

SERVES 16

BATTER

1/2 cup poppy seeds	2 cups flour
1 cup milk	2 teaspoons baking powder
1 1/2 teaspoons vanilla extract	4 egg whites
3/4 cup butter	1/2 cup seedless raspberry jam
1 1/2 cups sugar	

Soak the poppy seeds in the milk and vanilla overnight.

Preheat oven to 350°F. Grease two 9-inch, round cake pans and sprinkle with plain bread crumbs to evenly coat the sides and bottom.

In a standing mixer, cream the butter with the sugar. Add the flour and baking powder to butter mixture in small amounts, alternating with the poppy seed milk mixture. Mix well.

In a separate bowl, beat the egg whites until stiff. Fold egg whites into the batter and mix slightly.

Divide batter evenly between the two pans. Bake for 30-35 minutes or until a toothpick inserted in each center comes out clean. Remove from oven and cool completely.

Spread the raspberry jam between the cooled layers and refrigerate for several hours.

ICING

1 cup heavy cream
2 tablespoons confectioners' sugar
2 1/2 teaspoons vanilla extract

Beat the cream until thick. Add the sugar and vanilla and continue to beat until well combined. Spread on the top and sides of the torte just before serving.

BLACK TORTE
Tort Czarny

ALINA'S WEDDING CAKE

Peter's mother and father dated as students in Warsaw before World War II. When the hostilities began, Peter's dad joined the gallant Polish cavalry (to fight tanks on horseback), was inevitably and quickly captured by the Germans and was locked up for most of the war in a POW camp for military officers. Peter's mom was active in the Warsaw underground and ultimately escaped to Czechoslovakia just before the fall of Warsaw. By pure kismet, after the war they ran into each other during a rainstorm on a muddy street in a displaced persons camp in Germany. The romance was rekindled and they eventually married. They had nothing but each other. Peter's mom grew her own wedding bouquet and baked her own wedding cake. The recipe was given to her by her landlady and she had never baked anything in her life.

SERVES 16
Note: European tortes are usually served in small slices since they can be quite rich.

BATTER
5 egg yolks
2 cups confectioners' sugar
1 1/2 cups black walnuts, ground
2 teaspoons baking powder
3/4 cup flour, sifted
4 egg whites
plain bread crumbs

Using a standing mixer, beat the egg yolks for 3 minutes, add the sugar in small amounts while beating, and beat for 5 more minutes. Whip the egg whites until stiff. Combine walnuts with baking powder and flour. Fold the dry ingredients alternately with the whipped egg whites, a small amount at a time, and mix everything lightly.

Divide the batter equally between two 9-inch, round cake pans which have been greased or buttered, and sprinkled with bread crumbs. Bake at 350°F for 30-35 minutes, or until a toothpick inserted in the center of each pan comes out clean. Remove from oven and cool completely.

(recipe continued at right)

(recipe continued from left)
ICING
2 cups heavy cream
3 tablespoons strong instant coffee
1/2 cup powdered hot chocolate mix
   (dark is best)
1/2 cup black walnuts, chopped

Whip the cream, add the coffee and mix. Add the chocolate powder and beat until stiff and spreadable. Spread between the layers, on the top and around the sides. Sprinkle the top with chopped nuts. Refrigerate for at least 10 minutes before serving.

WARSAW FRUIT CAKE
Keks Warszawski

There are dozens and dozens of fruitcake recipes from all corners of the world. This classic version supposedly originated in Poland's capital. It is quite light, not-so-sweet and has a very easy hand with the dried fruit. It is very appropriate at holidays and with Sunday afternoon high tea, which was always popular among pre-war high society. A little rum or brandy drizzled over the top makes it truly sing.

YIELDS 2 loaves

BATTER
5 eggs
1 1/2 cups confectioners' sugar
2/3 cup butter, softened
1 teaspoon vanilla
1/4 cup milk
3 teaspoons baking powder
3 cups flour
3/4 cup candied orange rind, finely chopped
3/4 cup raisins
1/2 cup figs, finely sliced
1/2 cup prunes, finely sliced
1/2 cup walnuts, chopped
2 teaspoons cornstarch

Preheat oven to 350°F. Grease and flour 2 8x4-inch loaf pans. (see note)

Using a standing mixer, beat the eggs with the sugar for 7 minutes. In a separate bowl, cream the butter with the vanilla until light and fluffy. Beat milk into the creamed butter mixture. Add half of the flour and all of the baking powder to the creamed mixture and mix thoroughly. Fold in the beaten egg and sugar mixture, followed by the remaining flour. Mix the fruit and nuts with the cornstarch and fold into the batter.

Divide the dough evenly between the 2 loaf pans. The pans should only be about 1/2 full. Bake for 50 minutes or until a toothpick comes out clean. Serve with coffee, tea or a homemade cordial (see pages 92-93).

Note: Mini loaf pans may also be used. Divide batter between pans, filling each pan only half full. Baking time will be reduced to 30-35 minutes, depending on the size of your pans.

Walnut Ring Cake
Orzechowy Wieniec

SERVES 15

BATTER

4 eggs
2 cups confectioners'sugar
2/3 cup butter, softened
2 3/4 cups flour, sifted
3 teaspoons baking powder
1/3 cup rum
1 1/2 cups walnuts, chopped
1/2 cup chocolate chips

Preheat oven to 350°F. Grease and flour a 10-inch tube or bundt pan.

Using a standing mixer, beat the eggs with the sugar for 5 minutes at high speed. Add the butter in small amounts and beat an additional 3 minutes.

Add the flour and baking powder in small amounts, alternating with the rum. Beat 5 more minutes. Fold in the walnuts and chocolate chips.

Pour the batter into the prepared pan. Bake for 1 hour or until a toothpick inserted in the center comes out dry. Remove from oven and cool for 15-20 minutes before removing from pan.

ICING

1 1/2 cups confectioners' sugar
1/4 cup cocoa
2 tablespoons butter
4 tablespoons milk
whole nuts for garnish

Mix the sugar with the cocoa. Heat the milk to boiling and melt the butter in the milk. Add the sugar and cocoa to the milk and butter, and mix. Drizzle the icing over the cake and garnish with nuts.

APPLE RAISIN CAKE
Ciasto z Jabłkiem i Rodzynkami

For many generations of bakers, the flavors and aromas of apples, cinnamon and vanilla have always complemented each other marvelously. It's a combination seen in many baked goods, not only in Poland but in other countries as well. While baking, the aromas hit every corner of every nearby room and awaken every taste bud of anyone in sniffing range. Watch who will invent excuses to hang out near the oven and be the first in line for samples! This classic cake is that good! Plus, it's almost foolproof to make.

SERVES 16

BATTER

1 cup butter, softened
2 cups sugar
4 eggs
2 cups flour, sifted
2 teaspoons cinnamon
1 teaspoon vanilla
1 teaspoon baking soda
3/4 cup raisins
4 cups apple, coarsely grated
1 cup walnuts, chopped

Preheat oven to 350°F. Grease and flour a 10-inch, round springform cake pan.

Using a standing mixer, beat the butter with the sugar until creamy and pale. Add the eggs one at a time and beat an additional 5 minutes. Add the flour, cinnamon, vanilla and baking soda and beat 3 more minutes. Fold in the apple, raisins and nuts.

Pour batter into prepared pan and distribute evenly. Bake for 1 to 1 ½ hours or until a toothpick inserted in the center comes out dry. Remove from oven and cool for 15-20 minutes before releasing from pan.

HOLIDAY GINGERBREAD CAKE
Piernik Świąteczny

Polish gingerbread is a classic Christmas culinary tradition dating back to the 14th century when the crusaders first brought exotic spices back to Poland. There are dozens of varieties and each Polish cook has one or more favorites. Some have icing on top. Some have bits of dried fruit in the batter. Some are filled with a spread of jam between layers. Some are rolled and cut into decorative cookies (See Page 30). Some are served as bars or squares. Peter and Laura chose this recipe because it is a true classic and because it was a favorite of all their friends and neighbors who helped taste the goodies while Laura was testing. This version can be prepared well before Christmas and frozen until the big day.

YIELDS about 48 pieces

DOUGH

1 cup sugar	4 teaspoons butter
1/4 cup water, boiling	4 cups flour, sifted
3/4 cup honey	1 egg
2 teaspoons allspice	2 teaspoons baking soda
1 teaspoon cinnamon	1/3 cup water
1/2 teaspoon cloves	1 egg yolk, beaten
1/2 teaspoon nutmeg	

Place 2 tablespoons sugar in a medium saucepan. Brown the sugar over medium heat. Add 1/4 cup of boiling water and stir until sugar is dissolved. Add the remainder of the sugar, honey, spices and butter. Bring to a boil while stirring constantly. Remove from the heat and allow the mixture to cool.

Put the cooled sugar mixture into the bowl of a standing mixer with dough hook attachment. Add the flour, egg, baking soda and 1/3 cup of water. Knead the dough for a few minutes until the dough leaves the sides of the bowl and starts to form a ball. Cover the dough with plastic wrap and let stand for 20 minutes.

Preheat the oven to 350°F. Roll the dough out on a floured board and spread in a 12x15-inch buttered and floured pan. Brush the dough with the beaten egg yolk. Bake for 15 minutes.

Cool. Slice the baked cake through the middle into two equal layers widthwise.

FILLING

1/2 cup heavy cream
6 ounces chocolate, semi-sweet
1 teaspoon vanilla
1 1/4 cups confectioners' sugar
3/4 cup almonds, toasted and ground

(recipe continued at right)

(recipe continued from left)

Heat the cream in a medium saucepan to just boiling. Remove from the heat and add the chocolate. Let sit for a minute and then whisk until chocolate is melted and smooth. Add the remaining ingredients and mix well.

Spread the filling over one of the two layers. Place the second layer on top. Cover the top with plastic wrap, place a heavy object on top and let stand overnight. *Hint: Laura uses a bacon press or phone book and the purpose is to bond the layers into the chocolate filling.*

When ready to serve, cut the cake into small squares (about 2 x 2). Any extra pieces should be stored in an airtight container to prevent drying out. (They may also be frozen.)

Tip: this dessert is better after a few days so that the aromatic spices have time to infuse the cake thoroughly.

HARVEST CAKE
Placek Owocowy

Spring time brings an abundance of just-harvested fresh fruit. Right from the tree, they are aromatic, flavorful and beautiful for baking desserts. This traditional cake is very accommodating because it works well with almost any fresh fruit from farmers' markets or grocery stores. When the fresh ingredients go up in price this cake can also be made with canned or frozen fruit. Years ago, these fruit-based cakes were tied to the seasons, with peaches being best in the spring and some plums best in the early fall. But today, when fruit are grown all over the world and easily available to most of us on a year-round basis, we are no longer restricted to selected ingredients at specific times of the year. That gives our choice of menus more flexibility, even though this bit of progress takes away some of the excitement of anticipating fresh new flavors that become available with each new season.

SERVES 12

1 1/2 cups sugar
3/4 cup unsalted butter
1 1/2 cups flour
3 eggs
1 teaspoons baking powder
6 ripe, medium peaches, peeled, halved and pitted
3 teaspoons sugar
3/4 teaspoon cinnamon
Confectioners' sugar
breadcrumbs

Note: Use any flavorful fruit you wish, such as peaches, plums, apples, apricots, etc. For smaller fruit just increase the quantity.

Preheat oven to 350°F.

Using a standing mixer, cream sugar and butter. Add the eggs to mixture and beat well. Add the flour and baking powder and mix until totally incorporated. Put batter into a greased 9x12-inch pan sprinkled with bread crumbs. Place the fruit halves in rows on top of the batter, cut side down, about an inch apart. They will sink slightly.

Mix the sugar and cinnamon and sprinkle lightly over the top.

Bake for 50 to 60 minutes or until a toothpick inserted in the center comes out clean.

Cut into serving portions and sprinkle with confectioner's sugar just before serving.

These go really well with a small glass of homemade, flavor-infused vodka (see pages 92-93)

PINEAPPLE WALNUT BARS
Placek z Ananasem i Orzechami

DOUGH

3 cups flour, sifted
2 teaspoons baking powder
3 tablespoons sugar
1 cup butter
3 egg yolks
1/2 cup milk

Preheat oven to 350°F.

In the bowl of a standing mixer, mix the flour with the baking powder and sugar. Cut the butter into the flour until it resembles course crumbs. Mix the egg yolks with the milk and add to the flour. Knead the dough until all ingredients are incorporated well and dough forms a ball.

FILLING

5 cups crushed pineapple, drained
6 tablespoons cornstarch
1/2 cup sugar

In a medium saucepan, mix the pineapple, cornstarch and sugar and cook on low heat until the mixture thickens. Set aside to cool.

Line a 10x15-inch baking pan with parchment paper and butter the paper. Divide the dough into 2 equal pieces. Roll out the pieces of dough into rectangles, each large enough to fit in the prepared baking pan. Place one rectangle in the baking pan. Spread the pineapple mixture over the dough. Lay the second dough rectangle over the filling.

Note: for a more artistic presentation, cut the top layer of dough into strips and arrange in a pretty lattice design.

TOPPING

1 egg white, beaten
1 cup walnuts, chopped

Brush the top dough layer with the beaten egg white and sprinkle with the walnuts.

Bake for 40 minutes until golden brown on top. Remove from the oven. Cool on a baking rack. Cut into portions and serve.

EASTER CHEESECAKE
Sernik Wielkanocny

Cheesecakes are among the most popular desserts in Poland. One can find as many varieties as there are regions and towns in Poland. The traditional varieties that date back several centuries are a favorite during holidays such as Easter. They differ quite a bit from American versions because they are usually made with ricotta or farmer's cheese. These are drier and more crumbly than American cream cheese and thus yield a lighter, less dense filling.

YIELDS 32 portions

CRUST

1/3 cup butter	1 egg
1 3/4 cups flour	3 tablespoons sour cream
1/2 cup confectioners' sugar	3/4 cup seedless raspberry jam
1 1/2 teaspoons baking powder	breadcrumbs

Using the paddle attachment of a standing mixer, cut the butter into the flour until it forms coarse crumbs. Mix the egg with sour cream and add, then add the sugar and baking powder. Mix until all the ingredients come together into a soft dough. Refrigerate for 30 minutes.

Roll out 2/3 of the dough to fit a 9x12-inch pan, buttered and sprinkled with bread crumbs. Bake at 375°F for 10 minutes. The crust will be only partially baked. Remove from oven and cool. Spread the raspberry jam over the partially baked crust.

Note: if you wish to make a traditional decorative lattice on top of the cheesecake, reserve the remaining third of the dough and keep it cold until you are ready. If you've chosen to forgo the lattice, use the entire dough ball in the baking pan.

CHEESE FILLING

6 eggs	2/3 cup unsalted butter, softened
2 1/4 cups confectioners' sugar	2 1/2 tablespoons flour
1 1/2 teaspoons vanilla extract	1 1/2 pounds ricotta or farmer's cheese
2 teaspoons lemon zest	1/2 cup candied orange rind, finely chopped
2 teaspoons orange zest	1 egg white, beaten

Using a standing mixer, beat the eggs with the confectioners' sugar for 5 minutes at high speed. Add the vanilla, and lemon and orange zests. Combine the cheese with the butter and flour and add to the egg and sugar mixture. Fold in the candied orange rind. Spread mixture over the partially baked crust and raspberry jam.

Bake for 50 to 65 minutes or until the cake is firm. Remove and cool.

To decorate the top with lattice, remove the cake from the oven after the first 30

(recipe continued at left)

(recipe continued from right)

minutes, or as soon as the filling is firm enough to support the dough strips without sinking.

Form the remaining dough into thin, even rolls (like long straws) and place them diagonally across the top of the cheesecake in a criss-cross pattern. Brush the latticework lightly with a beaten egg white.

Note: for aesthetics, try to lay out the lattice rolls evenly parallel to each other, but don't worry if they break or don't quite stretch to the edge. Stretch and seal the breaks and they'll be just fine after baking – a few imperfections add rustic character to your cake.

Return the cheesecake to the oven and continue baking for an additional 20-30 minutes until the lattice is golden brown and the cheesecake is firm.

Krakow Cheesecake
Sernik Krakowski

This is one of Peter and Laura's favorite Easter desserts. It just may be the lightest and fluffiest cheesecake they've ever had. So full of delicious flavor and a pretty delight to admire on the table, this one is always a winner.

YIELDS about 20 pieces

CRUST

1 1/2 cups plain breadcrumbs
1/2 cup sugar
1/3 cup butter, melted

Mix all the ingredients for the crust together and spread over the bottom of a 9-inch spring form pan. Bake at 350°F for 8 minutes and set aside. The crust will be only partially baked.

CHEESE FILLING

1 1/2 pounds whole milk ricotta cheese
4 egg yolks
3/4 cup light cream
1 cup sugar
1/3 cup flour
1 teaspoon vanilla extract
zest of 1 orange
1/2 teaspoon lemon zest
2 tablespoons lemon juice
1 cup mashed potatoes
4 egg whites, whipped stiff

Using a standing mixer, beat the cheese with egg yolks and half of the cream until well combined. Add the rest of the cream, sugar, flour, vanilla, both zests and lemon juice and beat enough to combine all the ingredients thoroughly. Mix in the mashed potatoes and combine. Fold in the beaten egg whites and mix lightly until combined evenly.

Pour the cheese filling over the partially baked crust. Bake at 325°F for 1 hour and 15 minutes. Turn off the oven and leave the cheesecake inside, with the oven door partially open, for one hour.

Remove pan from the oven and let the cheesecake cool completely. Remove from spring form pan. Garnish with powdered sugar and very thin strips of orange rind before serving.

GRANDMA'S CHEESECAKE
Sernik Babci

YIELDS 36 squares

DOUGH FOR CRUST

1/3 cup butter
1 3/4 cup flour
1/2 cup confectioners' sugar
1 1/2 teaspoons baking powder
1 egg
3 tablespoons sour cream
breadcrumbs

Using the paddle attachment of a standing mixer, cut the butter into the flour until it forms coarse crumbs. Add the sugar, baking powder, and egg mixed with sour cream. Mix until all the ingredients come together in a soft dough.

Roll out the dough to fit a 9x12-inch pan, buttered and sprinkled with breadcrumbs. Bake at 375°F for 10 minutes. Dough will be only partially baked.

CHEESE FILLING

5 eggs
2 cups confectioners' sugar
1 1/2 teaspoons vanilla extract
1 pound farmer's cheese, ground (may substitute ricotta cheese)
1/2 cup butter
1 cup mashed potatoes
2 teaspoons baking powder
1/4 cup raisins
1/4 cup orange zest
1/2 teaspoon nutmeg (optional)

Using a standing mixer, beat the eggs with the confectioners' sugar for 5 minutes at high speed. Add the vanilla and nutmeg. Combine the cheese with the butter, potatoes, baking powder and add to the egg and sugar mixture. Fold in the raisins and orange zest. Spread mixture over the partially baked crust.

Bake for 45 to 60 minutes until firm and golden brown.

Cool and cut into 2-inch squares in the pan.

STRAWBERRY MERINGUE TART
Skubaniec

Unexpectedly, this dessert became an instant favorite of Peter and Laura's friends and neighbors who tasted plates and plates of goodies during the whole time this book was being assembled. It's actually quite light and the slight crunch of the meringue, matched to the sweet strawberries and thin crust, really excites the taste buds. These days, strawberries are available all year around so there's no excuse for not trying the recipe anytime and for any occasion. If you're looking for a grateful hug, this dessert will rise to that challenge.

YIELDS 32 squares

DOUGH
1 cup butter, softened
2 cups flour
2/3 cup confectioners' sugar
4 egg yolks
3 tablespoons yeast (1 ounce)
1 tablespoon flour

Preheat oven to 350°F. Butter and flour a 10x15-inch pan.

Using the paddle attachment of a standing mixer, cut the butter into the flour until it resembles course crumbs. Add the sugar and mix. Mix in the egg yolks. Combine the yeast with 1 tablespoon flour and add to the dough mixture. Knead the dough until it just comes together.

Moisten your fingers and spread the dough evenly over the prepared pan. Bake for 10 minutes and remove from the oven. Reduce oven temperature to 325°F.

TOPPING
6 tablespoons bread crumbs
5 cups strawberries, hulled, sliced thinly and well drained
6 egg whites
2 1/4 cups sugar

Sprinkle partially baked crust with the bread crumbs. Distribute the strawberries evenly on top of the bread-crumbed crust.

Beat egg whites until soft peaks form. Add the sugar gradually, continuing to beat until stiff. Spread the egg whites over the strawberries. Return the tart to the oven and bake for an additional 30 minutes or until the meringue is light gold in color. Cool slightly and cut into squares. Best served slightly warm.

Note: the baked strawberries are juicy so this tart doesn't store very well. Left over portions will get soggy but that process can be slowed if stored cold.

CHERRY TART
Placek z Czereśniami

Peter and Laura love the way this dessert looks on the dinner party table. It's elegant and somewhat unique because cherries are not found in Eastern European pastries as often as in the U.S. This tart is very comforting and one of the authors' favorites among all the desserts in this volume.

SERVES 8

DOUGH

1/2 cup butter, softened	2 egg yolks
1 1/4 cups flour	1 teaspoon vanilla extract
1/4 cup sugar	

Preheat oven to 350°F. Using the paddle attachment of a standing mixer, cut the flour into the butter until it resembles coarse crumbs. Add the sugar and mix. Add the egg yolks and vanilla and mix until dough comes together. Spread the dough evenly on the bottom and up the sides of a 9-inch, round tart pan with a removable bottom. Bake for 25 minutes. Remove from oven and cool.

FILLING

8 ounces ricotta cheese	1 teaspoon lemon juice
1/2 cup confectioners' sugar	2 tablespoons milk

Combine the cheese with all the remaining filling ingredients and mix well. Spread the filling over the cooled tart crust.

TOPPING

3 tablespoons cornstarch	1 teaspoon butter
1 cup cold water	4 cups cherries, pitted and halved
2/3 cup sugar	2 tablespoons sliced or slivered almonds, lightly toasted
1/2 teaspoon almond extract	

Note: pitting the cherries carefully is an absolute must to make sure no one breaks a tooth. This is not a fun task but can go much easier and quicker with a less-than-ten-buck cherry pitter found in the gadget department of any good kitchen store, or online.

In a saucepan, mix the cornstarch with cold water, add the sugar and bring the mixture to a boil over medium-high heat while stirring constantly. Simmer for a few minutes until mixture thickens. Add the almond extract and butter. Fold in the cherries and combine. Cool slightly. Spread over the cheese-filled tart shell. Sprinkle top with the toasted almonds.

RHUBARB CRUMBLE
Placek Rabarbarowy

By itself, rhubarb is quite tart. On the grocery shelf, it looks like red celery and if you taste a fresh piece while prepping, your lips will definitely pucker up. But when cooked down and sweetened, it adds a very fresh and bright tang to any recipe. When Laura first tested this dessert, the consensus of the tasting "experts" was to go bolder and add more rhubarb to the cake. This may become one of your "go-to" desserts for company because the recipe is very straightforward and the bright flavors will end your meal with a nice contrast.

YIELDS 32 squares

CAKE BATTER
1 1/4 cups butter, softened
3/4 cup sugar
1 1/2 cups flour
1 1/2 teaspoons baking powder
1/2 cup milk
4 eggs, separated
1 teaspoon vanilla extract
1 1/4 pounds rhubarb, cut into ¼ to ½-inch pieces

Preheat oven to 350°F. Butter and flour a 10x15-inch pan.

Using a standing mixer, mix the butter and sugar until pale and creamy. Mix the flour with the baking powder and add to the butter alternately with the milk. Add the egg yolks one at a time, beating constantly. Add the vanilla.

In a separate bowl, beat the egg whites until stiff. Fold into the dough and mix lightly. Spread the dough evenly in the prepared pan. Distribute the rhubarb pieces evenly on top of the batter.

TOPPING
1/2 cup butter, softened
1 cup flour
1/4 cup brown sugar, lightly packed

Mix the butter and flour until it resembles coarse crumbs. Add the sugar and mix well. Sprinkle the crumb mixture over the top of the rhubarb.

Bake for 40 to 45 minutes or until a toothpick inserted in the center comes out clean. If the crumb topping starts to brown too quickly, place a piece of aluminum foil over the top of the cake. Remove from oven. Cool and cut into portion-sized squares.

FILLED DONUTS
Pączki

This is the single most requested dessert for inclusion in this book. As Laura and Peter traveled up and down the East Coast, signing their first book, at every stop folks were regaling them with stories about the *Pączki* made a long time ago by their *Babcias* or *Mamas*. They are much like an American filled donut, only made with unique aromatics and different fillings. In Poland, the most traditional filling is rose hips jam. They also resemble the famous beignets from Café Du Monde in New Orleans, but larger and filled with fruit jam.

In Poland, *Pączki* are traditionally prepared for "Fat Tuesday," which is just before Ash Wednesday. Generations ago, they were a great way to use up all the lard, sugar, eggs, and fruit jams, most often rose hips, which could not be consumed during Lent. Today, there are modern *Pączki* festivals all over the world and in the U.S. wherever there are large Polish-American communities, such as in Chicago, New York, Detroit or Cleveland.

Peter didn't get to eat a lot of *Pączki* while growing up. Before the days of dough beaters and standing mixers, his mother thought they were too much work. Truth be told, they do take some time and practice to perfect but they are absolutely worth it. Laura mastered the dough on her second or third batch and everyone who sampled the output of her recipe testing said they are way better than any mass-produced donut from the store – including the *Pączki* sold in Polish delis up and down the East Coast. As far as Peter and Laura are concerned, these are absolutely on par with the *Pączki* they sampled on their last trip to Poland. *Hint: they will be best when eaten slightly warm* – so much love, so aromatic, so delicious!

YIELDS 18 to 24, depending on size

1 1/2 cups milk	1 teaspoon orange zest
4 1/2 teaspoons active dry yeast	1 teaspoon vanilla
1/2 cup vanilla sugar	3 1/2 cups all purpose flour
1/2 cup softened salted butter (one stick)	1 1/2 cups cake flour
1 large egg	Oil for frying, (canola is a popular choice)
3 large egg yolks	Raspberry, plum or rose hips jam for filling
1 tablespoon vodka	Confectioners' sugar for sprinkling on top
1 teaspoon salt	

Warm the milk to between 105°F and 110°F. Add the yeast to the warm milk, stir to dissolve and let stand.

In the bowl of a standing mixer, cream the vanilla sugar and butter until fluffy. Beat in the egg and egg yolks, vodka, salt, vanilla and orange zest until thoroughly incorporated. Mix the two flours together and add a little at a time, alternating with the milk and yeast mixture, and mix for approximately 5 minutes. Replace

(recipe continued at right)

(recipe continued from left)
the paddle attachment with the dough hook and knead until smooth. Dough will pull away from the sides of the bowl.

Notes: mixing two types of flour adds lightness to the dough. That little bit of vodka added to the dough actually has a purpose. As it evaporates, it prevents the oil from absorbing deep into the dough.

Flour your hands and place dough in a greased bowl, turning to coat all sides with the grease. Cover and let the dough rise in a warm place until it has doubled in size. This process may take over an hour. Punch the dough down, recover and let it rise for a second time. The second rise may take 25-30 minutes.

Place the dough on a lightly floured cutting surface. Pat or roll the dough to a ½ inch thickness. Cut the dough into 3-inch rounds using a biscuit or cookie cutter. Re-roll scraps and cut. Lay the cut donuts on a cookie sheet lined with parchment or wax paper. Cover and let them rise for about 20 minutes, until doubled in size. *Note: be sure to spread them out enough to allow for doubling in size without touching.*

Place oil in a deep fryer or large, heavy pot such as a Dutch oven (oil should be about six inches deep) and heat to a temperature of 350°F. It is extremely important to keep the oil temperature consistent, so a thermometer is helpful. If the oil is too hot, the outside will brown before the inside is done and if the oil is too cool, the *Pączki* will absorb the oil and be too greasy.

Carefully place the *Pączki* top side down in the oil a few at a time. Fry for 2 minutes until the bottom is golden brown. Turn the *Pączki* over and fry an additional 2 minutes until golden brown. Cut one open to be sure it is cooked through. Adjust your cooking time as needed.

Drain the *Pączki* on paper towels or brown paper.

Pączki filled with rose hips jam are the most traditional variety in Poland and usually glazed and topped with candied orange peel. But any good jam will do. Poke a hole in the side and using either a pastry bag or pastry injector, squeeze in about one to two tablespoons of jam. Dust the completed *Pączki* with confectioners' sugar or glaze.

GLAZE
2 1/2 cups confectioners' sugar
2 tablespoons softened butter
6 tablespoons hot water

Mix confectioners' sugar and softened butter. Gradually add the water until the mixture is smooth and silky. Glaze should be thin but not runny. More water may be added if necessary to create the appropriate consistency.

PAPAL CRÈME CAKE
Kremówki Papieskie

It is hard to imagine how a casual remark can elevate a tasty but common pastry into global stardom. In 1999 Pope John Paul II, on a visit to his boyhood hometown of Wadowice, made an offhand comment about a childhood memory of the sweet taste of a crème cake called *Kremówki*. He and his schoolmates used to buy them in a pastry shop in the main town square. This slight comment went viral, to use today's terms, and resulted in a huge impact on the entire Polish confectionery industry. On the very next day, *Kremówki* became the rage and appeared on the shelves of all the local bakeries. The news spread like a gospel through all of Poland and ever since the confection has been known as the Papal Crème Cake.

YIELDS 9 generous portions

PASTRY LAYERS
2 sheets frozen puff pastry dough

Just thaw the frozen puff pastry sheets. Preheat the oven according to package directions. Roll the pastry sheet slightly to erase the fold lines. Score (do not cut all the way through) each pastry sheet into 9 sections. Scoring will make the sections easier to cut when serving.

Tip: don't let the pastry sheets thaw to room temperature; otherwise, they will become too sticky to work with.

Place the pastry sheets on a cold baking sheet and bake according to the package directions until golden. Remove from oven and allow to cool completely.

CRÈME FILLING
4 cups whole milk
2 teaspoons vanilla extract
1 1/2 cups sugar
2/3 cup flour
1/8 teaspoon salt
12 egg yolks

Add the vanilla extract to the milk and scald (bring just to boiling). In a second pot, a heavy saucepan, combine the sugar, flour, salt and egg yolks and whisk until there are no lumps. Slowly stir in the hot milk and vanilla. Cook over a medium to low heat, stirring constantly to keep the crème from sticking to the bottom of the pan. Bring mixture to a low boil, reduce the heat to low and continue to boil for 3 minutes while stirring constantly.

Pour the crème into a fresh bowl to cool. During the cooling process, stir the mixture occasionally.

(recipe continued at right)

(recipe continued from left)
ASSEMBLY
Place one layer of the baked puff pastry in the bottom of a rectangular baking pan. Pour the pastry crème evenly over the layer, about one to two inches high. Place the second layer of puff pastry on top of the filling and press down lightly. Refrigerate at least 1 hour until filling has stiffened somewhat. Using a very sharp, thin knife, gently cut into squares along the scored markings. Dust the cakes with confectioners' sugar. Use a thin spatula to transfer each portion to serving plates.

Note: when cutting the squares it is inevitable that some of the crème filling will run out. For a prettier appearance, use an icing spreader to push the crème back between the layers of puff pastry and to smooth out the edges.

POPPY SEED ROLLS
Makowiec

No collection of heritage Polish desserts would be complete without a recipe for Poppy Seed Rolls which are such an iconic part of traditional Polish Christmas menus. Peter does not remember one Christmas without a Poppy Seed Roll on the table, even if it was not home-made. As Peter and Laura travel to many Polish festivals with their first book, **Polish Classic Recipes**, this confection is one of the first that everyone asks about and one of the favorites everyone remembers their mother or grandmother baking for Christmas.

YIELDS 4 rolls

DOUGH

3/4 cup butter	1 teaspoon vanilla extract
5 cups flour	1 tablespoon grated lemon rind
1 cup confectioners' sugar	2 tablespoons dry active yeast
2 eggs	1/4 cup warm water
2 egg yolks	1 tablespoon sugar
1/2 cup sour cream	

Cut the butter into the flour with a knife or pastry cutter and then rub in with your fingertips. Add the confectioners' sugar to the butter and flour. Mix the yeast with 1/4 cup of warm water and sugar. Add the rest of the ingredients including the yeast mixed with the sugar. Using a standing mixer, knead the dough for about 5 to 8 minutes until the dough is smooth and elastic.

FILLING

1 pound raw poppy seeds	1/2 cup honey
1/2 cup chopped almonds	1/4 cup candied orange rind
8 tablespoons butter	1 teaspoon grated lemon rind
1 cup sugar	1 egg, beaten
1/2 cup golden raisins	2 egg whites
1 teaspoon vanilla extract	

Simmer the raw poppy seeds in a pot of water (enough to cover) until soft, about 40 minutes. Stir frequently. Drain the poppy seeds using a fine sieve. Press as much water as you can from the seeds. Place the seeds in a bowl and set aside for a couple of hours or overnight to allow excess moisture to evaporate. Grind the poppy seeds in a food processor for about 4 minutes.

Add the chopped almonds to the poppy seeds and grind for a few seconds. Melt the butter in a saucepan or skillet. Add the poppy seed mixture, sugar, raisins, vanilla, honey, candied orange and lemon rinds, and cook over medium-low heat for 10 minutes. Cool slightly and add the beaten egg. In another bowl, whip the egg whites until stiff peaks form and fold into the filling mixture. Let cool.

Divide the dough into 4 equal parts. Roll each piece into a rectangle. Spread each

(recipe continued at left)

(recipe continued from right)
rectangle with an equal amount of filling leaving a one inch margin from each edge. Starting at the long end, roll the dough into a log and seal the ends.

With the seam side down, place the rolls on a non-stick or a greased cookie sheet.

Place the rolls in a warm oven to rise. Let stand until the rolls double in size, about 1 hour.

(Option if using the glaze: brush the rolls with milk and sprinkle with poppy seeds before baking.)

Bake at 350°F for 30 minutes. Cool.

Rolls may be served as-is from the oven, or decorated using either the icing or the glaze.

ICING

2 cups confectioners' sugar
1/3 cup lemon juice, or rum

Mix the confectioners' sugar and lemon juice or rum. Spread on the rolls and decorate with candied orange rind.

GLAZE

4 tablespoons apricot preserves
1 tablespoon lemon juice
1 tablespoon rum

Heat the preserves and lemon juice on medium-high until bubbling. Pour mixture through a fine sieve to remove any remaining fruit pieces, reserving the liquid. Stir the rum into the liquid. Brush the glaze mixture over the roll and scatter almonds on top.

PLUM DUMPLINGS
Knedle ze Śliwkami

These dumplings are quite hearty and were often eaten in Poland as a somewhat sweet main course for dinner. Traditionally, this particular dough is based on mashed potatoes. When it encases a sweet plum, that first bite releases a mouthful of delightful flavors that instantly beg for more. When Laura first tested the recipe, Peter had not tasted these dumplings for many years. But the first bite immediately recalled the memory of his childhood when his mom made them as an occasional special treat. They were a special favorite of Peter's dad for whom these dumplings were a tradition in his childhood home in Poland.

YIELDS 12 Dumplings

DOUGH
2 cups potatoes, peeled, boiled and mashed
1 cup flour
1 egg
Salt to taste

Mix all of the ingredients by hand until they form a soft dough.

Note: it is best to mix the dough by hand because the use of mixers or food processors can overwork the potatoes.

Using your floured hands, divide the dough into 12 portions.

FILLING
12 small Italian plums or 6 larger plums, halved
Sugar & Cinnamon, mixed (if needed)

Wash and dry the plums. With a sharp knife, cut a deep gash into each plum and gently remove the pit, being careful not to tear the flesh of the plum. If using larger plums, cut them in half and remove the pit. Depending on the sweetness of your fruit, add about half a teaspoon of mixed sugar and cinnamon to the center of the fruit where the pit was.

ASSEMBLY
Using your floured hands, flatten the dough pieces and then mold the dough around the plum or plum half. Be sure to cover all of the plum evenly with dough to ensure the fruit does not fall out of the dough when cooking.

(recipe continued at left)

(recipe continued from right)
COOK
Fill a large pot with salted water and bring to a boil. Gently place 3 or 4 dumplings in the boiling water. With a spatula, gently make sure they don't stick to the bottom of the pot. Cook for 8-10 minutes depending on the size of your dumpling. Gently remove the dumplings to a warmed platter.

TOPPING
1 1/2 tablespoons breadcrumbs
1 1/2 tablespoons butter, melted
1/3 cup confectioners' sugar

Sauté the breadcrumbs in melted butter until golden brown. Pour over the dumplings. Sprinkle with confectioners' sugar and serve.

CREPES WITH SWEET CHEESE
Naleśniki z Serem

YIELDS 10

CREPES
1 cup milk
2 eggs
1 cup flour
1/2 cup water
1/2 teaspoon salt
3 tablespoons vegetable oil

Mix the milk with the eggs, flour, water and salt in a blender. Heat a 6 to 7-inch non-stick skillet or crepe pan and brush or spray the pan with oil. Pour a small amount of batter into the skillet. (For a 6-inch pan use a little less than 1/3 cup of batter per crepe). Immediately tilt the pan around so the batter will completely cover the bottom of the pan. When the crepe is slightly browned underneath, using a very thin spatula or turner, flip it over and cook on the other side. Remove the crepe from the pan and stack on a plate with a sheet of wax paper between each crepe to prevent sticking. Continue this process until all batter is used.

CHEESE FILLING
1 cup ricotta cheese, creamed
1/4 cup sugar
1 teaspoon vanilla
1 tablespoon grated orange or lemon rind

Cream the ricotta cheese using a mixer or food processor. Add the remaining ingredients to the cheese and combine. Stuff each crepe with a small amount of the filling and roll it up into a cigar-like shape. Or, you can fold the crepe in four like an envelope.

SWEET WHITE SAUCE
1/3 cup confectioners' sugar
1/2 cup sour cream

Whisk the confectioners' sugar with the sour cream. Top the crepes with a small amount before serving. Garnish with your favorite berries.

Note: as a change of pace, crepes may also be filled with your favorite fruit preserves or jam. Spread each open crepe lightly with jam and fold in four. Warm and serve. Alternatively, the crepes are also wonderful when topped only with fresh, seasonal berries or this blueberry sauce.

(recipe continued at left)

(recipe continued from right)
BLUEBERRY SAUCE
2 pints fresh blueberries,
    washed and stemmed
1/2 cup vanilla sugar, or more to taste
3 teaspoons fresh lemon juice
2 teaspoons cornstarch

Combine all the ingredients in a small saucepan and cook over medium heat until the sugar dissolves and the berries start to boil and pop, releasing their juices – about 3 to 4 minutes. Cool partially, pour over each crepe and serve.

DRIED FRUIT COMPOTE
Kompot z Suszonych Owoców

At the end of a festive fall or winter meal, when the leaves have turned and the outside air is crisp, a small dish of compote, served in shimmery Polish crystal; glittering in the light of tall, delicate candles; makes an elegant and comforting statement that you care about your guests. In Poland, compote was considered a cold-weather dessert because it takes advantage of summer fruit harvests that were preserved by drying, then brought back to life in sugar, water and spices. In these modern times, compote can be offered year-round due to the ready availability of dried fruit in the grocery stores. This is a traditional Christmas Eve dessert and the legend goes that it was originally made with twelve different fruits for the twelve apostles. From his earliest childhood, Peter remembers being served a dish of compote along with a savory ginger heart cookie, piece of aromatic baba and slice of poppy seed roll – the most important desserts of Christmas Eve.

YIELDS 8 servings

1 1/2 pounds mixed, dried fruits such as plums, apricots,
  figs, cherries, apples, pears, raisins, cranberries
5 cups water
5 whole cloves
2 cinnamon sticks
zest of 1 lemon
2/3 cup sugar, more or less to taste

Combine fruit, water, cloves, cinnamon, zest and sugar in a 6-quart saucepan and bring to a boil.

Lower the heat to simmer, cover the pan and cook for about 20 minutes or until the fruit is tender and the syrup has thickened slightly.

Cool completely. Compote may be stored in the refrigerator for up to 1 week.

STRAWBERRY KISSEL
Kisiel Truskawkowy

As soon as Peter and Laura saw the recipe for this dessert, Peter remembered it from his childhood. His mother made it a lot because it was quick and easy, inexpensive (most post-war immigrant families lived on very tight budgets) and had an intense, fresh-fruit flavor that has stayed with Peter even until now. He loved tasting Laura's first batch and their 2-year-old granddaughter Lucy loved her first spoonful – she smiled and opened wide for more. Enough said?

YIELDS 8 half-cup portions

1 1/2 pounds strawberries, hulled and sliced
1/4 cup sugar
1 1/2 cups water
1/2 cup sugar
4 tablespoons cornstarch
1/2 cup cold water

In a traditional blender or using an immersion stick blender, puree the strawberries with the 1/4 cup sugar and set aside.

In a saucepan, mix 1 1/2 cups water with ½ cup sugar. Heat mixture to boiling and remove from the heat. Dissolve the cornstarch in ½ cup cold water and stir into the sugar-water mixture. Return to the heat and boil, stirring constantly. Remove from heat, add the strawberry puree and mix well.

Cool the mixture slightly and portion into cool, single-portion bowls or into one large serving bowl. Cool in the refrigerator until firm, which may take several hours.

Serve drizzled with cream or with a dollop of whipped cream.

Poached Pears in Sauce
Gruszki w Sosie

These elegant pears are typical of the not-so-sweet fruit desserts that are characteristic of Polish cuisine. They are among Peter and Laura's favorite desserts for fancy dinner parties because the pears can be easily dressed with sauce for a very striking presentation that always impresses. Laura especially appreciates this dish because the pears and both sauces can be prepared a day or two ahead of time and put on hold in the fridge. Your guests will appreciate their lightness and big flavors as a great way to end a big meal. Peter likes his pear either with a glass of semi-sweet dessert wine or a small cup of very strong espresso.

SERVES 4

4 large pears, any variety
1 quart water
1 1/2 cups sugar

Put the water and sugar in a pan large enough in which to stand your pears. Simmer for 10 minutes. Peel the pears and remove the core from the bottom, leaving the stem intact. (Alternatively, you may halve the pears and core them). Add the pears, standing straight up, to the simmering sugar syrup. Bring syrup back to simmer and cook the pears for about 12 minutes or until just tender but not mushy. Remove pan from the heat and let the pears cool. Just before decorating, remove the pears from the syrup and pat dry.

VANILLA SAUCE

1/3 cup sugar	2 egg yolks, slightly beaten
2 tablespoons cornstarch	2 tablespoons softened butter
1/8 teaspoon salt	2 teaspoons vanilla
2 cups milk	

Mix sugar, cornstarch and salt in a medium saucepan. Combine milk and beaten egg yolks and gradually stir into the sugar mixture. Cook over medium heat, stirring constantly, until the mixture thickens and boils. Remove pan from the heat and stir in the butter and vanilla.

With the sauce at room temperature, pour a small pool on the serving plate and stand a pear upright in the middle of each pool.

CHOCOLATE SAUCE

1/2 cup light cream	4 ounces finely chopped bittersweet chocolate
1 tablespoon sugar	1 teaspoon vanilla
1 tablespoon unsalted butter	

Add cream, sugar and butter to a medium saucepan. Bring the mixture to a boil. Remove pan from the heat and immediately add the chocolate. Let the chocolate

(recipe continued at right)

(recipe continued from left)

stand in the cream mixture for a minute. Whisk the mixture until the chocolate is completely melted and the mixture is smooth. Add the vanilla and whisk. With the sauce at room temperature or slightly warmer, drizzle over the top of each pear.

Serve chilled or at room temperature. For color, garnish with mint leaves, lemon peel, cinnamon sticks, berries or whatever you have to flavor-match the dish.

Be prepared for compliments!

Notes:

1) The pears and sauces can be prepared ahead of time but hold off assembly until shortly before serving; otherwise, the chocolate will run off the pears.

2) For bigger flavor, spice up the sugar syrup by adding a piece of a cinnamon stick, 6 whole cloves, half a vanilla bean and the julienned zest of one lemon to the pan with water and sugar.

COFFEE CUSTARD
Krem Kawowy

When Laura first tested this dessert, she and Peter were both struck by the rich and decadent intensity of the coffee flavor and by the silky smoothness of the texture.

Throughout Poland, as in much of Europe, coffee shops are seen on most street corners and in many town squares. They are to the Europeans what pubs are to Londoners and street vendors to New Yorkers. They are an important fabric of social life where customers sit and take their time over a cup of coffee and maybe a sweet. Many Poles still like their coffee brewed the old-fashioned way by putting a spoonful or two of grounds into a glass tumbler and filling it with boiling water. If you are a coffee lover, then you will fall in love with this dessert.

SERVES 4

5 egg yolks
1 egg
6 tablespoons sugar
2 1/4 cups heavy cream
2 tablespoons instant espresso powder
1 1/2 teaspoons vanilla
whipped cream

Preheat oven to 300°F.

With a whisk, beat the egg yolks and egg with the sugar until smooth. Set aside.

In another bowl, pour ½ cup of cream over the espresso powder and vanilla extract. Whisk until the powder is fully dissolved. Add the remaining cream and whisk again until thoroughly blended. Combine the contents of both bowls and whisk gently to mix completely.

Note: using a whisk to mix these ingredients by hand will avoid overbeating and adding too much air to the unbaked custard.

Pour the mixture into 2/3 cup-size baking ramekins. Fill the ramekins almost to the top because the custard will shrink a bit while baking. Place the ramekins in an oven-safe baking dish and place into the oven. Then, gently pour some boiling water into the baking dish, about ¾ of the way up the sides of the ramekins. Be careful not to splash any water into the custard.

Place dish in the oven and bake for 40-50 minutes or until the custard jiggles slightly. Remove the baking dish from the oven and place on a rack to cool. Leave the ramekins in the water until custards are firm and the water has cooled.

Serve the custard in their original baking ramekins, topped with a dollop of whipped cream.

POPPY SEED BREAD PUDDING
Makówki

This is a very traditional dessert similar to a British trifle. The yeastiness of the bread, and characteristic tastes of the poppy seeds, honey and dried fruits evoke images of 14th and 15th century Polish nobility enjoying their bread puddings washed down with glasses of Honey or Plum Liqueur (see pages 92-93).

SERVES 12

2 cups raw poppy seeds (see note)
2 cups whole milk
2 cups heavy cream
1 tablespoon butter
3/4 cup honey
1/3 cup rum
1 teaspoon almond extract
1 teaspoon cinnamon
2 cups mixed dried fruits (raisins, candied orange rind, apricots, figs, dates, cherries, or cranberries)
1/4 cup walnuts, chopped
1/4 cup almonds, sliced
1 loaf challah bread, cubed or sliced (or any sweet yeasty bread)
whipped cream

Simmer the raw poppy seeds in a pot of water (enough to cover) until soft, about 40 minutes. Stir frequently during this process. Drain using a fine sieve. Press as much water as you can from the seeds. Grind the poppy seeds in a food processor for about 4 minutes. *Note: for a quicker version, substitute 12 to 14 ounces of prepared poppy seed filling found on the baking aisle of better grocery stores.*

Combine the milk, heavy cream and butter in a large pot and bring almost to a boil over medium-high heat. Add the honey, rum, almond extract, cinnamon, dried fruits and nuts to the pot while stirring constantly. Simmer the mixture on medium-low heat for 10 minutes, stirring occasionally.

Remove the pot from the heat and add the poppy seeds (or prepared poppy seed filling). Stir well and let it sit for 10 to 15 minutes until slightly thickened.

In a glass serving bowl, alternately layer the poppy seed mixture and bread, starting and ending with the poppy seed mix (3-4 layers). Cover the bowl and refrigerate overnight.

Serve in a parfait dish or large wine glass, topped with whipped cream and garnished with nuts or any of the dried fruits.

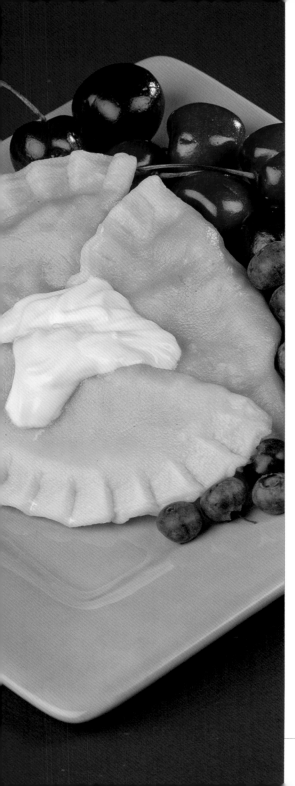

Sweet Pierogi
Pierogi Słodkie

This recipe has been tested to perfection. The dough is so much lighter than what you normally see in mass-produced pierogi. You may want to practice a bit, just to get the thickness and cooking times down pat.

YIELDS 45 to 50 three-inch pierogi

FILLING (2 cups)
2 cups fruit: pitted cherries; peeled, chopped apples; or blueberries
1/2 tablespoon flour
1/2 cup water
1/4 cup sugar
1/4 teaspoon cinnamon
2-4 tablespoons bread crumbs (optional)

Toss the fruit with the flour and combine with water and sugar in a saucepan. Bring the fruit mixture to a slow boil, reduce heat and simmer for about 10 minutes until fruit is soft and water is almost evaporated. Remove from heat. Add cinnamon and mash slightly. Cook again on low until thickened, about 5 minutes. The optional bread crumbs may be added to thicken the fruit mixture, if needed. Let cool while you make the dough.

DOUGH
2 eggs
2/3 cup milk
1/4 teaspoon salt
2 cups flour
1 egg, beaten with 1 tablespoon of water, for sealing

Whisk together the two eggs, milk and salt. Stir in half of the flour until incorporated, then add the rest and continue stirring. When the mixture forms a thick, sticky dough, place it on a floured surface. Using additional flour, knead the dough until smooth, supple and soft, but not sticky. Form the dough into a ball, wrap it in plastic and let it rest for 15 minutes.

Take half of the dough and roll it out as thin as possible on a floured surface. It should be almost translucent, about 1/8 inch. Cut the dough into 3 or 4-inch rounds or circles.

ASSEMBLING

Place a small amount of filling in the center of a dough round. Be sure to leave about a 1/4 inch edge around the entire dough round. Too much filling and the pierogi won't fold in half properly, or the dough will tear or could burst during cooking.

Brush the edges of the dough round with the beaten egg. The egg wash "glues" your edges together. Fold the dough in half into a half-moon shape. Pinch the edges of the rounds firmly together using your fingers or the tines of a fork. Tight sealing will keep the edges together during cooking. Keep the finished pierogi covered with plastic wrap as you are filling the rest to prevent the dough from drying.

COOKING

Bring a large pot of well-salted water to a boil. In batches, place the pierogi in the water. When the pierogi float to the top, continue to boil for 10 to 12 minutes. Cooking time will vary according to the size and thickness of your dough. Test the first one to see if the dough is cooked through, similar to cooked pasta. Remove the pierogi with a slotted spoon and drain.

TOPPING

1 cup sour cream
1/2 cup confectioners' sugar

Whisk sour cream with the sugar. Top the pierogi generously with sauce. Best when served warm.

STORING

For storing and serving later, pierogi (without the topping) may be partially cooked and frozen individually on a covered tray, then stored in portion-sized, plastic freezer bags up to 6 months. To reheat, just drop them in simmering hot water for a few minutes.

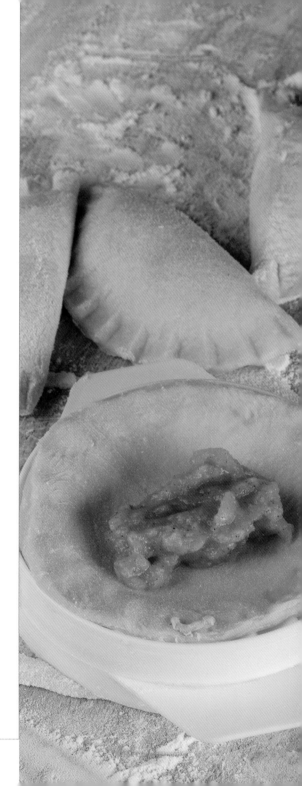

ADULT BEVERAGES

Not only do Poles love to eat, but some enjoy sipping an adult beverage every now and then. Many traditional desserts go better when served with a little alcohol. A glass of chilled dessert wine or Plum Liqueur will arouse your taste buds and enhance the flavors of a babka or a chocolate cookie. Our ancestors knew that a little alcohol with food helps the digestion and enhances the flavors…but always in moderation! Peter's father loved to infuse lemon peel or orange peel in vodka, and the results were delicious. There are many flavored alcohol products on the market today, but Peter has always thought making his own is more interesting. It's easy and they're great conversation starters at parties. These four recipes are very traditional and will be smoother when made with a good-quality Polish potato vodka.

HONEY LIQUEUR
Krupnik
YIELDS about 4 cups

1 cup honey
1/2 cup water
1 teaspoon vanilla
1/4 teaspoon nutmeg
1 tablespoon cinnamon
1 teaspoon lemon zest
2 1/2 cups vodka

In a pot, mix together the honey, water, vanilla, spices and lemon zest. Bring to boil, cover and simmer lightly for 5 minutes. Add the vodka, heat and serve immediately in small tumblers or liqueur glasses. *Note: Be careful that the glass is thick enough not to crack from the hot liquid.*

CHOCOLATE CREAM CORDIAL
Likier Czekoladowy
YIELDS about 4 portions

5 egg yolks
3/4 cup confectioners' sugar
1 1/2 tablespoons dark chocolate syrup
1 2/3 cups vodka
1/4 cup heavy cream

With a mixer, beat the egg yolks and sugar until thick and creamy. Add the chocolate syrup and vodka. Beat for another minute until well integrated. In a separate bowl whip the cream and then whisk in to the liqueur. Serve in small glasses with dessert. Best cold.

PLUM LIQUEUR
Śliwówka

YIELDS about 36 two-ounce pours

2 quarts vodka – 100 proof if you have it
1 cup sugar
3 cinnamon sticks

2 to 3 quarts plums, not fully ripe
 (Italian plums are great)
4 whole cloves

Rinse the plums, cut in half, remove the pits and place them in a sterilized, one-gallon jar. Pour one half of the vodka into a large saucepan. Warm up the vodka slowly and add the cloves and cinnamon sticks. Stir in the sugar slowly and completely dissolve by whisking or stirring. Let the vodka cool to room temperature, then pour into the jar over the plums. Add remaining vodka. Seal the jar tightly and place it in a dark place, such as a pantry or closet. Forget about it for one to three months. Break it open for Christmas and serve in small liqueur glasses as an aperitif with sweets. Save the plums if you wish to add a few pieces to your traditional Christmas compote. (page 81)

CHERRY CORDIAL
Wiśniak

YIELDS about 12 two-ounce pours

1/2 pound fresh dark cherries
1 cup sugar
2 cups quality vodka

Slit each cherry on two sides and remove the pit. Place cherries in a sterilized, 1-quart jar. Pour the sugar over the cherries (do not stir or shake the jar). Slowly add the vodka down the side of the jar until full, but leave a 1/2 inch space at the top. Make sure the cherries are completely covered with vodka, but again do not stir or shake the mixture. Seal the jar tightly and put in the pantry or closet at room temperature for 3 months. After 3 months, strain the liqueur and it is ready to serve in small liqueur glasses. Keep the cherries, if you wish, for a tasty compote with a kick.

INDEX OF RECIPES

ACKNOWLEDGEMENTS

We are very grateful to all the support and encouragement received from so many friends and family, especially to:

Blue Rose Pottery, Ft Mill SC, for being so generous with your beautiful Polish pottery to complement our desserts on these pages http://bluerosepottery.com

Bob Rock, for your photographic wizardry to showcase these dishes in the best possible light

Cheryl Butler, for gleefully tasting just about everything that came down the hill

Christina and BJ, our daughter and son-in-law, for providing honest feedback, and for allowing us to tempt your diets

Dan Dalcin, for styling some of these desserts to look great, in spite of long hours at the stoves

Jeanine Smith, for your steady hand with a piping bag

Kit Wohl, for creating a grand template for the entire Classic Recipes series

Michael Lauve, for your inspired and creative designs

Paul J. Watkins, for helping keep the "grammarians" happy

Polish Pottery Mart, Savage Mill MD, for lending pretty Polish ceramics

Zoe Kiklis, for opening the doors to your china closet

Bob Rock, *Food Photographer*
www.bobrock.com

Dan Dalcin, *Food Stylist*